SO YOU WANT TO PLAY BY EAR?

4.50

SO YOU WANT TO PLAY BY EAR?

A Practical Guide to Improvisation

Claire Liddell

Stainer and Bell

First published in Great Britain 1980
by Stainer & Bell Ltd
82 High Road, London N2 9PW

ISBN 0 85249 582 X

Printed in Great Britain by Galliard (Printers) Ltd, Great Yarmouth

Contents

For 'JCL'
whose encouragement
has been invaluable

What it's all about

This book has been prompted by the many people who have come to me with a common wail:

I can play the piano — a bit of Mozart and even an easy Chopin waltz — but I can't harmonise anything by ear when my friends ask me, or even when I'm alone.

But anyone can. YOU CAN.

This is aimed at YOU — and all those other people who have a beginner's knowledge of the keyboard and who want some fun from it.

FOUR FIRST PRINCIPLES:

1   There is a 'hoodoo' that discourages most of us from trying to make up music if we are not born composers: but young children make up tunes quite happily and you probably did as a child. Improvising tunes *and harmonising them* is not difficult if you use your ears.

2   Magic results will not come overnight but if you look on it all as an adventure — not as a 'subject' — persevering can be a pleasure.

3   Everything depends on keen listening. We all suffer from lazy ears as they are constantly washed with sounds not meant to communicate with our minds: we usually let music float over us without focussing it in our brains.

4   It is vital that your brain hears a sound inside your ear *before* you play it.

Step 1: The Family Circle

The first step on the way to harmonising is to look at your basic equipment of

KEYS

Keys are interesting and you must be on easy terms with them. You will recognise them as friends by their individual 'voices' as you know your other friends on the telephone. The sounds of keys are known by the number of sharps and flats which they use.

It does not matter how many sharps or flats a key has. As you memorise and listen they will become as familiar as any group of your acquaintances; no need to be nervous of 'E flat major'.

To recognise the sound of each key in your mind, play the major scales, up to three sharps or three flats, once every day (one hand will do); listen to the sharps or flats particularly and remember them in the way they reach your ear. The scales are printed on page 78 for you to read but remember that you should memorise them so that you play them *by ear*. The first thing you need when you want to PLAY BY EAR is to be able to play these major scales by ear: first from memory based on the sight and the fingers, then by listening to the notes and recognising their sounds.

Look now at the Family Circle of the House of Keys. Key C is at the bottom. The Sharp keys climb up the left half; the Flat keys climb up the right half. Where the same keynote on the piano has two names the keys overlap and sound the same: F sharp and G flat are identical twins in sound. Play them thinking what they *look like*; then play them listening simply to their sound.

Ex. 1

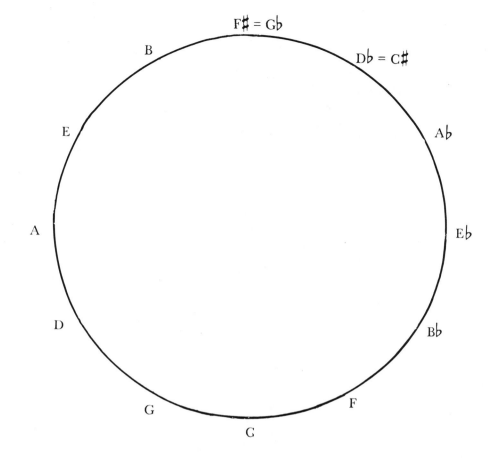

Splitting up the Family Circle in two, here are the keys sounding with up to three sharps or flats in the key signature. Sharp keys climb up the left side; flat keys up the right.

Ex. 2

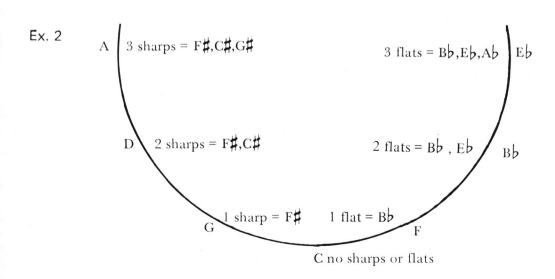

Step 2: Relatives

By now you should be able to pick out our Major Keys without having to search for them. The equipment also contains Minor Keys. To recognise *their* voices up to their signatures of three sharps or flats, play them once every day (one hand will do): listen to the sharps *and* flats particularly — notice some scales have both — and remember the way they reach your ear.

Unlike major scales, each of which can be played in one way only, minor scales have two versions: the Melodic Minor and the Harmonic Minor. Their names simply tell you that one is used for melodies (tune-hearing) and the other is used for harmonies (chord-hearing). You will find them on pp 79/80; again memorise them so that you can play them *by* ear. Listen to the different sound of the Melodic Minor as it comes down after going up; and listen carefully to the sixth and seventh notes of the Harmonic Minor, the same going up and coming down. Play the last four notes of each harmonic minor scale time and time again until you get the 'snake-charmer's' sound in your ears.

Each major key is related to a minor key in much the same way that we have relatives in most family circles. You must be able to recognise the major-minor relationship when you hear it before you can begin to hear it in your harmony.

This is how you can recognise the relatives by eye. To find the minor key related to C major (which has no sharps or flats as you know by now) count three semitones (that is, black and white notes on the piano) *down* from C:

Ex. 3

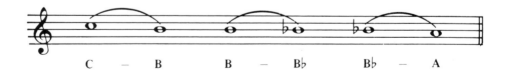

C — B   B — B♭   B♭ — A

The note you land on is the keynote of the Relative 'minor' of C: A for 'A minor'. Now if you play the melodic minor of A minor going down, listen to the sound as a tune; then, play the scale of C major going down (starting on the C first above the A) and listen to its tune *by comparison*. Play them alternately for some time and you will begin to hear their relationship.

Try tracing a relative the other way round, as if you had met the minor key first. Count three semitones *up* – playing them on the piano – from the minor keynote D:

Ex. 4

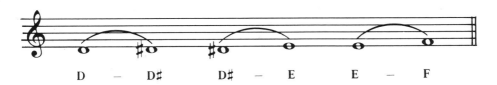

D — D♯   D♯ — E   E — F

F is the keynote of the relative major: F major. Play the scales of F major and D melodic minor downwards and listen to the relationship as you did for C and A minor. After several hearings, the relationship between the scales may not seem so strange.

All this is a lot to digest, so take your time over it. Listen keenly to appreciate the different sounds of major and minor. You may find yourself hearing the difference emotionally – for many people a minor scale has a 'sadder' sound than a major, particularly the 'snake-charmer' harmonic minor; but be content for now if you can at least hear that there *is* a difference.

A warning about the *look* of minor scales when they become keys for a piece of music. Look at the D melodic minor scale going down on page 80: it has the same notes as the F major scale going down on page 78 and shares one common black note, B♭. The key 'signature' at the beginning of a piece will be the same for D minor as F major; you cannot tell by *looking* at the piece in which of the two keys it is but if you play it or listen to it your *ear* should now be able to tell you.

Don't fall into the trap of thinking that C major is related to C minor. It isn't and your ear will tell you so. Remember, then, that a piece in a minor key uses the *same* key-signature as its relative major although its key note is different:

Ex. 5

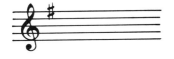

means either G major or E minor

means either F major or D minor

Step 3: Picking out a tune

Before you can start to harmonise you must be able to pick out a tune with your right hand on the piano. Your experience of listening so far will help you. To set about it, let us take a simple test case: how do you go about playing 'Quand Trois Poules' *alias* 'Baa, baa, Black Sheep' *alias* 'Twinkle, twinkle little star'?

1 Sing it out loud.
2 Sing it in your head. Does it sound major or minor?
3 Take C for the starting note and try to play the first phrase at the keyboard. Don't worry if you play a wrong note, but correct it by listening carefully to the tune in your head.
4 Play it again, stop, and sing it out loud again.
5 Write the notes (heads only if you like) on manuscript paper as you play them through again:

Ex. 6

Ask your ear to notice the big gap between the first two and the second two notes, two Cs and two Gs. Then notice the much smaller gaps between the remaining notes. These gaps are easy to see but you must learn to **hear** the difference between them as well.

Sing the phrase once more and listen to the gaps. These spaces between notes are another part of your equipment:

INTERVALS

If this seems boring, think for a moment. You should now be able to play the phrase not only from memory but, at the same time as you sing it, simply by using your ears. Just for fun, alter a note as you sing the tune: can you hear the wrong note you are singing? Now play the tune again and try to play the wrong note when it comes in your singing. Compare this with the original tune. If you can do this with one tune you are on the way to playing any other tune by ear and getting it right first time.

Try a few more; never mind about writing down the rhythm at this stage but use manuscript to get used to seeing the sound as you hear it.

Sticking to white notes on the piano, practise playing 'intervals'. The interval between the first pairs of notes in your first written phrase is, counting inclusively, five notes:

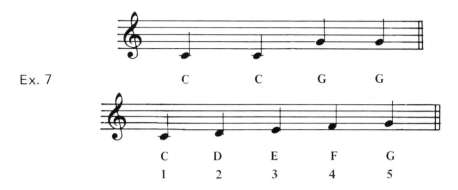

Ex. 7

Remember, always include all the notes in your counting. Write:

Ex. 8

then write the notes in between:

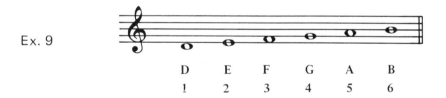

Ex. 9

and count the lot. The interval in Example 7 is 5 notes, called a '5th'; so Example 8 is a '6th'.

Still sticking to the white notes of the piano, play the first note of each of these intervals, try to hear the second note, sing what you think it is, then play it. If you were right, your ear is coming on. If not, your eye might help if it recognises the 'interval' and your ear remembers the sound of the interval. What are these three intervals called? Answer on page 81.

Ex. 10

Step 4: What key am I in?

When you have written down a few tunes you have played by ear – the tune could just as easily be one you have made up entirely, your own 'composition' – you must learn to recognise its key. This is where the understanding of scales you have practised until now is so valuable.

Supposing you have picked out 'The First Nowell' and you find that your hand and your ear as you first sing it landed on F♯ as the starting note, you will have written something like this.

Ex. 11

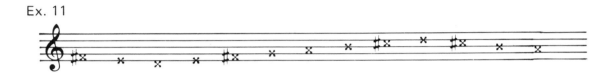

Now you need both ears and eyes for detective work: the sharps are your clues. Ask yourself:

1 Is this in a major or minor key? Sing it through and ask your ear. It should by now tell you 'major'. Remember that you can practise recognising major or minor by singing to yourself anywhere – in the bath, on the train, in a car – any tune that comes into your head, any time.
2 What are the black-note clues? **Sharps.** So the tune is in a key on the left hand side of the Family Circle of major keys.
3 Which sharps has it got? F♯ and C♯.
4 Which major key in the Circle has two sharps? D major.

The case is solved: you have played the tune of 'The First Nowell' **BY EAR** in D major. But did your ear do it alone or did your eyes help your deduction? Your eyes will tell you that no other *major* key has only these two sharps. If your ear had told you the tune was 'minor', though, what would the key have been? Look at page 79 and let your mind help. (Answer on page 81.) Here is a trickier case to solve. What is the key of this?

Ex. 12

After you have done your detective work on the lines of the previous page, turn to the answer on page 81.

Beware of false trails. When a tune has neither sharps nor flats, your eye will tell you it is in C major or A minor; but your ear may recognise it is not. Take this well-known tune:

Ex. 13

There are no black-note clues. As before, ask your ear 'major or minor'? As you play it through several times, ask your ear if it hears one note with a stronger 'pull' than the others every time it sounds, as if it was a kind of homing signal guiding it to a safe landing? In this tune, the 'homing' note is marked with a cross. If your ear does not recognise it to begin with, play it several times – listening *carefully* – until you can persuade yourself that 'G' is the strong note and, therefore, the key. Once you can agree, pick out the whole tune to check. When you write it out, put in the black-note 'signal' as if there had been one in the tune – G major has one sharp, F♯, which is shown in the 'key signature'. If it had been there, your eye would have helped you solve the case sooner, but without your ear in the first place you could not be sure.

Ex. 14

Recognising the key of a melody that shows no sharps or flats to the eye takes practice . . . but trust your ears. Once you can recognise keys, you can begin to add harmonies and really PLAY BY EAR.

Step 5: It's too high

One last piece of tuneful deduction before you start adding chords as you play: you may find that the tune you have picked out on the piano is too high or too low for you or your friends to sing.

If your friends feel that a tune in the key of C is too low, how do you set about changing it?

1 Play 'John Peel' on the piano by ear using only white notes.
2 What key are you playing in? C major.
3 Listen to the first note. What is it? E.
4 Where does your starting note belong in the scale of C major? The third note:

Ex. 15

5 If you want to put the tune up, take the keynote up. One tone higher will mean the key of D. So you want to play in D major. The opening note is, as you know, the third in the scale. What is the third note in the key of D major? F (and don't forget it!) **Sharp.** So you can play the tune one whole tone higher in D major — remembering that C and F are both sharp and that the starting note will be F♯. If your friends want the tune lower, try playing it in A or even G (though you will more likely find they want it higher, say in E flat). Take your courage in one hand and try to play 'John Peel' in all the keys up to three sharps or flats, starting for example on C♯ for A major. Apply the 'question and answer' method any time you don't know what to do next and let your ear confirm every answer.

Interlude I

At this point, it's good to have a rest.

If you are a gardener, you could say you have cleared the ground, done the pre-liminary spadework and can now dream about the exotic plants you are going to grow. Every gardener enjoys deciding the many different choices of flowers or vegetables to plant but knows that the time between planting and the appearance of the shoots — let alone fruits — is a time for patience and faith.

So have in mind the kind of pieces you would like to play. Are you aiming at any or all of:

> Dance Music?
> Community Songs?
> Hymns and Carols?
> All the 'Evergreens'?
> Your own world-beater?

The choice is yours. Think ahead and every step you take will mean more and be clearer.

Step 6: Growing chords 1

Each note of a scale is a 'root', using a gardening term borrowed by musicians. To trace the growth of common chords on the notes of a scale above the roots:

1. Play and write the root note C.
2. Play and write the note which sounds three steps above it (remembering to count the 'gap' inclusively). Play the two notes together.
3. Play and write the note which sounds three steps above note 2. Play the three notes together.
4. Play and write the note which sounds four steps above note 3. Play all four notes together. (If your hand is too small, play the root with the left hand and the three notes above with the right hand.)

So the chord built on the note of C (in the *key* of C major) is:

Ex. 16

Remember, when you count intervals between notes of a scale you must include the notes at each end of the gap:

E to G = E, F, G = 3 notes = gap of three = an interval of a third.

Since the first note of the scale of C major is C, this is 'Chord 1' in the key of C major. In this way, you can grow all the chords of all the keys from their scale roots. Here are all the chords of the scale of C major:

Ex.17

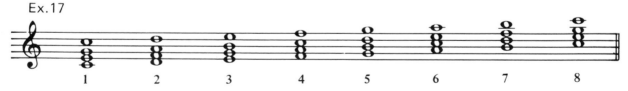

Try growing the chords of the scale of G major, then D major, and A major; then the flat keys of F major, B♭ major, and E♭ major. The same method of growing applies to all the keys. (See page 82 to check *your* chords.)

It is most important also to practise playing the chords of the scale with the left hand. If your left hand is too small, play the top note with the right hand and the other three with the left hand. Both hands must have a sure knowledge of these chords.

Try the chords of keys up to three flats and three sharps with the left hand, too. (Check these 'bass' chords with page 83.)

Step 7: Numbering chords 1

From now on, every chord will be referred to by *number* as well as by *name*.

In the key of C, the chord grown on C – C, E, G, C – is called 'Chord 1', as it grows from the first note of the scale of C major.

But the chord grown on C in the key of G major – still the same C, E, G, C – will be called 'Chord 4' in that key, as C is the fourth note in the scale of G major. If you find this hard to understand at first, do not be disheartened. Ask yourself:

1 What is Chord 4 in D major?   2 What is Chord 5 in C major?

Play both chords. Your ears will tell you they sound alike.

Practise all the chords in the first three sharp and the first three flat keys, thinking as you play; 'I am in key . . .; this is Chord X in the key of . . .'. Just to check again: in C major, Chord 5 is the chord on G (G, B, D, G): You have **not** gone into the key of G major; you are playing the chord G in the key of C. Chord G is Chord 5 in the key of C, but Chord 1 in the key of G.

THIS DISTINCTION IS VITAL

Here are the chords of the scales of C and G again with the three most important chords numbered:

Ex. 18

Chords 1, 4 and 5 will be the basis of all your harmonies until your ear teaches you more exotic sounds. Practise these three chords alone, in all the major keys up to three sharps and three flats.

It is good to have a definite 'feel' about the identity of these three chords and to recognise their relationship *by listening*. You can think of them, if you like, as three members of a family. Chord 1 is the 'mother'; without her there would be no family, that is, no scale and therefore no key. Chord 5 is the 'father'; he has a commanding position and has something extra up his sleeve, providing for the future. Chord 4 is the 'only child' at this stage, completing the inner family circle. This is one way to get that family feeling which you must have to harmonise well.

Step 8: Beginning to harmonise 1

We are going to take a tune and put chords underneath it. The tempo will be slow to begin with, but you must make sure your ear understands every development. Select a tune without too many notes for a start. A nursery rhyme is often good material for your first experiments, but some popular tunes can soon take its place.

Take the basic tune from the early steps again, this time in G major, beginning:

Ex. 19

1   Pick out the first eight bars on the piano until you can play them easily by heart.
2   Write these bars down, being careful to add the key signature. Do not despair –
    you will not need manuscript paper much longer.

Here are the first eight bars in the key of G, divided into 'bars' by the vertical bar lines; these also show where the accents lie:

Ex. 20

Always, when you have decided on a tune, practise Chords 1, 4 and 5 in the key you have chosen, so that your fingers and ears get used to the basic material again. Now play the lowest note eight notes lower with the left hand, leaving a gap between your two hands. Practise all three like this and listen to the new, open sound. The left hand is playing the root from which the chord still grows. These are the only chords you need for the moment:

Ex. 21

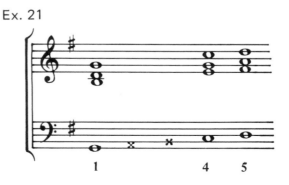

20

Since the key is G major and the first two notes are both G, you can expect that these two notes would happily take Chord G in G major: Chord 1:

Ex. 22

Play the chord several times to get it into your ear.

Bar 2: The two notes D, on sight, look as if you should play Chord D (in G major, Chord 5):

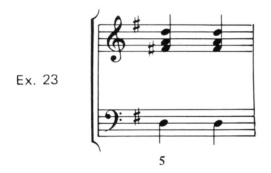

Ex. 23

But D is also in Chord G (in G major, Chord 1). So, by experiment with your fingers on the notes of the chord (G–B–D–G), you can arrive at the top note D but keep your left hand on the root: G.

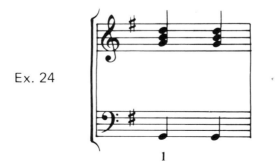

Ex. 24

The only way to decide is to use your ear. Is (a) or (b) better here?

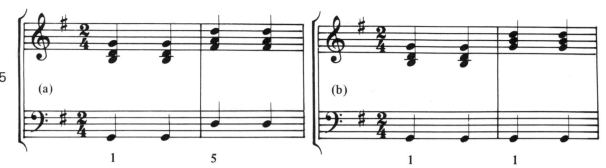

Ex. 25

Notice that you do *not* ask yourself about chords in isolation, but only as they relate to one another. Your ears may not wish to decide between (a) and (b) for the moment . . . or they may tell you clearly which they prefer.

Bar 3: The two notes E are only found in one of your three chords (see example 21) — Chord 4. But here, again, the note in the tune must be at the top and you must experiment with your fingers to put it there . . . still keep your left hand on the root. You can only end up with:

Ex. 26

This leaves your ears to decide between:

Ex. 27

(a)

or:

(b)

22

Perhaps you are still undecided . . .?

Bar 4: This has one long D, so the problem is the same as bar 2. Do you harmonise it with Chord 1 or Chord 5? Try both and you will have to ask your ears to choose between:

Ex. 28

and:

Ex. 29

If you ask your friends to confirm your ears, you will be most likely to end up with Ex. 29.

Play Ex. 29 again: does it sound a bit 'thick' and 'four-square'? You may like it this way, but, if you wish to lighten it, learn that you need not repeat a harmony under repeated notes unless you want to. Try:

Ex. 30

Notice that the root in bars 2 and 4 also moved up eight notes to lessen the space between hands. Only your ears can guide you in refinements like this. Good advice, though, is:

Always use chords sparingly and don't feel you have to harmonise every note of a tune

Looking back at example 20, harmonise the rest of the tune. Here are questions to ask to help you:

Bar 5: Three Cs. In which Chord –1, 4 or 5 – is there a C?
Bar 6: Two Bs. In which Chord – 1, 4 or 5 – is there a B?
Bar 7: Two As. In which Chord – 1, 4 or 5 – is there an A?
Bar 8: Long G. There is a G in Chord 1 and in Chord 4. Which do you prefer?

Remember that you must ask your ear to decide only in relation to the rest of the piece.

When you have solved the whole piece to your ear's satisfaction, look at page 84 and see if you agree. Remember that you must always be willing to try a sound and, if it seems 'wrong', change it. If you find others also think one of your sounds is 'wrong' when you think it is 'right' you can either stick to your guns (in this case, your ears) or – by analysing alternatives with your brain as in the examples above – offer an alternative.

Finally, you can experiment by adding notes in between those of the tune without altering the harmony, like this:

Ex. 31

This reinforces the advice given opposite: if you had started to harmonise the tune as it now sounds with its added notes you would have harmonised only one note in four! See how you can 'decorate' the rest of the tune.

Step 9: Growing chords 2

It is time to look again at the minor keys in the equipment. Chords are built in the same way as the majors in Step 6. Look back now to Step 2 and remind yourself of the two minor scales and their relationship to majors. Build Chords 1, 4 and 5 in A minor. Chord 1 is easy, using the intervals of a third and a fifth above the root:

Ex. 32

Practise Chord 1 in all the minor keys up to three sharps or flats. The scales on pp 79/80 will remind you what the notes of the chord will be. Then play the chord with the root in the left hand and experiment with the order of notes in the right hand as you did in Step 8. To start you off:

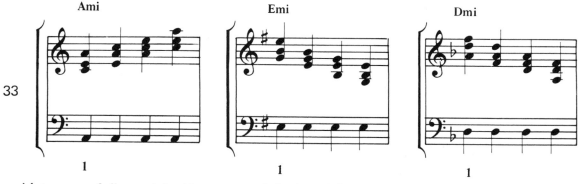

Listen carefully and *feel* how your right hand finger stretch varies.

Chord 4 gives your ear a choice, depending on whether you choose the interval of a third above the root from the melodic or the harmonic minor scale. A melodic minor:

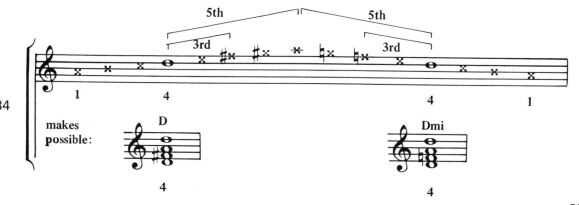

But A harmonic minor:

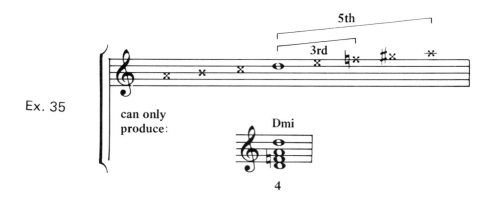

Ex. 35

can only
produce:

The same applies to Chord 5. A melodic minor:

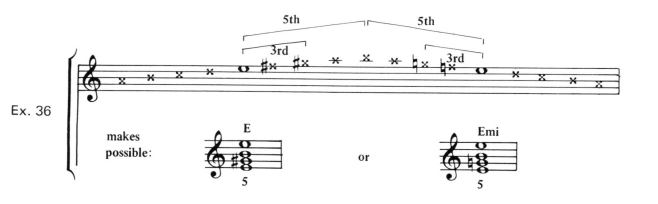

Ex. 36

makes
possible:

or

But A harmonic minor:

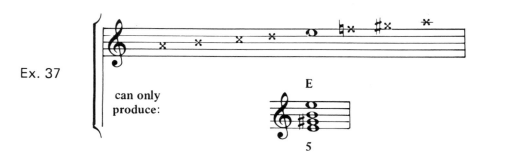

Ex. 37

can only
produce:

As you have probably guessed, in playing by ear you will normally harmonise with the 'harmonic' minor but there *may* be times when your ears tell you that a tune needs Chord 4 or 5 in the alternative provided by the melodic.

Practise Chords 4 and 5 as you did Chord 1 in all the *harmonic* minor keys. The scales on pp 79/80 will remind you again of the notes but try picking out the intervals *by ear* first. Now experiment with both hands for the different right hand stretches:

Another sentence to remember:

In harmonic minor, Chord 4 is minor but Chord 5 is major.

Step 10: Beginning to harmonise 2

In Step 8 you harmonised a tune in G major. What is the relative minor of G major? E minor. What is the key signature of E minor? One sharp. Remember that related minors have the same key signature as their majors (see page 11). Pick out the beginning of the carol 'We Three Kings' using the same method as before:

1   Sing it out loud.
2   Sing it in your head. Does it sound minor?
3   Take B for the starting note and pick out the tune at the piano.
4   Play it again, stop, and sing it out loud again.
5   Write the note heads on manuscript paper as you play them through again.
6   Try to write it in rhythm. It will look like this:

Ex. 39

As always, practise Chords 1, 4 and 5 in the chosen key. (In this case E minor.) Use the 'swinging' rhythm to practise on, like this:

Ex. 40

When you are confident in playing this exercise by ear look at the tune on your manuscript. Play the first bar and find one chord only to harmonise it, remembering that you do not have to harmonise every note. Which chord is it: 1, 4 or 5? Play the tune with its chord, using your right hand in the way you practised in the last exercise. You will be playing something like this:

28

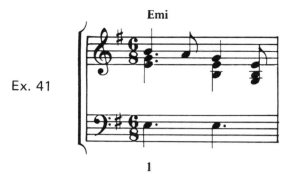

Ex. 41

Never mind if you had some different arrangement of notes; all that matters is that you played the tune with Chord 1 by ear.

Play the bar again and go *straight on* to the tune of bar 2. See if your fingers will find chords instinctively for bar 2. If not, practise your 'singing' exercise on the three chords and listen as you sing the tune to yourself. Can you find a chord for the beginning of the bar yet? Keep trying, without looking at the notes on paper. By now, you must have the answer: Chord 5, followed by Chord 1.

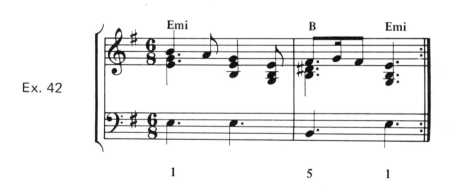

Ex. 42

Notice again that Chord 5 is a major. B major is Chord 5 in E minor. For fun, play the phrase again making Chord 5 minor (that is, playing D♮ instead of D♯) and listen to the difference. You can always amuse your ear like this, and it's not unattractive: you might even like it!

The tune repeats these two bars, then goes on like this:

43

Try finding two chords for bar 5. Your ears and fingers will tell you Chords 1 and 4. Bar 6 will puzzle your ear. In which chord – 1, 4 or 5 – is there a B? Play both (1 and 5), straight after playing bar 5 again. Which do you prefer? You may not know yet so play on to the second half of the bar. Remember, the tune (or melody) uses the *melodic* minor. What chord has two out of the last three notes in it? None of your harmonic minor Chords 1, 4 and 5. Try Chord 5 as the minor chord you played for fun: B minor (B, D♮, F♯). Doing things for fun can lead to new discoveries for your ear! Bars 5 and 6 may now be sounding like this:

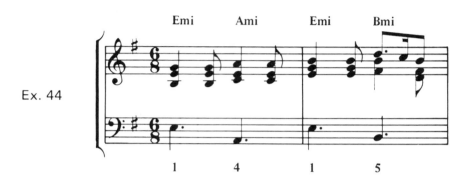

Ex. 44

This is not the *only* harmonisation. If your ears have given you something different, listen carefully to the difference and then decide for yourself.

Bar 7 may need three chords, marked x in the tune. Apply the same deductions from experimenting at the piano and you will end with this harmonisation of the whole tune (with your own variants if you prefer them).

Ex. 45

Step 11: Numbering chords 2

In Step 7, you have read that Chord 5 has something extra 'up his sleeve'. That something extra is another note which can occasionally be played in addition to the notes of Chord 5 **or instead of one of them**.

Play Chord 5 in G major:

Ex. 46

Count *seven* notes up from the root of the chord (D): remember always to count the root as 'one'. Playing the notes starting on D, you will arrive at the note C. Now play Chord 5 again (a) adding the note C and (b) using it instead of the top D:

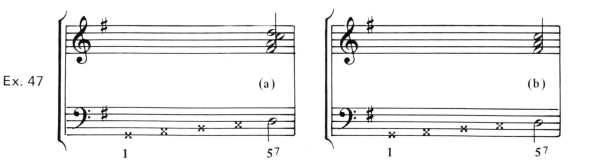

Ex. 47

(a)

(b)

This, as you see is called 'Chord 5⁷' or — because its root is D — 'D⁷'. (If you know anyone who plays the guitar, listen to 'D⁷' on the guitar then play it at the keyboard, letting your ears compare the sound.)

Find and practise Chord 5^7 in all the keys up to three sharps and three flats. Experiment with different places to put 'the seventh' like this:

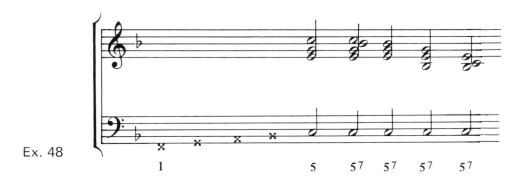

Ex. 48

Remember that guitarists call these chords after their root, so that in Example 37 above 'Chord 5^7 in the key of F is also called 'C^7'. What is 'Chord 5^7 in the key of D' called? Answer, 'A^7'. Most popular songs and folk tunes have guitar chords added nowadays. See if this helps to fix the 'sound of the seventh' in your ears.

Also remember that any harmony must be listened to **only as it relates to another** (see page 22). Now, therefore, try substituting the Chord '5^7' for '5' in a tune you have already harmonised. In our example tune, it has this effect in the last four bars:

Ex. 49

Play the whole tune with Chord 5 and then Chord 5^7 in the last bar but one, until you are sure you can hear the difference exactly.

The 'extra' note – the seventh – in 5^7 also means that you can think again when you ask yourself 'in which chord is there . . .?' (as you did on page 24). In bar 5 of the example tune are two Cs. So now you can ask yourself (remembering that the key is G):

In which chord – 1, 4, 5 or 5^7 – is there a C?

The answer is now two-fold: 4 *and* 5^7. When you asked the question on page 24, you could only answer '4'. Re-harmonise the tune with this in mind and see if your ear likes the change. The more chords you learn to hear the more flexible your choice becomes.

Here is one possible harmonisation of the whole tune to compare with yours:

Ex. 50

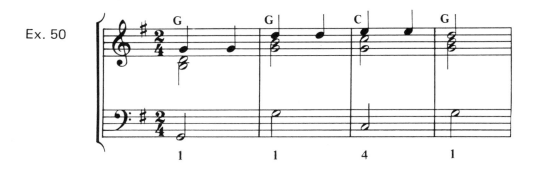

(continued)

Ex. 50 (continued)

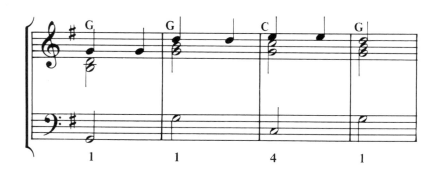

Interlude II

Before anything seems to be getting too complicated, re-check your steps so far. Above all 'you want to play by ear'. So you must be a critical listener. Do not be satisfied with the first sound that seems acceptable but try alternatives **until your mind is satisfied with what your ear tells it.**

Looking again at the possible harmonisation overleaf, note that the chord in bar 10 **could** have been Chord 4 but Chord 5^7 is preferred. In bar 12, the **chord** could have been Chord 5^7 but Chord 5 is preferred: the reason is that the ear tells the mind that Chord 5 is stronger and that Chord 5^7 seems to want to prolong the line rather than end it. In bar 16, the seventh is added late: the ear told the mind it moved the music along better and makes Chord 1 in bar 17 even stronger. The same reasoning led to both chords in bar 23.

Examine this reasoning with your own ear and apply similar reasoning to all your own harmonising. Soon you will learn to trust your ears and brain with the chords you have used so far. Only when you are really confident, take the next step — going 'pianistic'.

Step 12: Going pianistic 1

You have learned that you should not harmonise every note but be sparing with your harmony. To use the medium of the piano you should look at music by those composers who had that particular instrument in mind. They started composing for the 'new' instrument in the eighteenth century and one of them gave his name to one of the most effective 'pianistic dodges' of all time: Domenico Alberti's bass, or simply 'The Alberti Bass'.

So far your left hand has only played the root of your chords whilst the right hand played the rest of the chord *and* the tune. Partly because music can move too quickly for the right hand to play the chords with three notes or more at once, you can begin to make your playing by ear even more like the music of Alberti, or even Mozart and Haydn.

To do this, give only the tune to the right hand, and make your left hand play the chord — from its root upwards — but 'broken up' into a pattern of successive notes instead of playing them all together.

The chord of G major can be 'broken up' in many ways. Experimenting with rhythm, in the left hand:

Ex. 51

Apply one of these to your familiar major tune:

Ex. 52

Bars 1, 2, 4, 6 and 8: show Chord 1 in piano terms.
Bars 3 and 5: are left to themselves to avoid being fussy.
Bar 7: is the Chord 5⁷ in piano terms.

There are fewer notes; it is easier to play; and it *sounds* like piano music. Play it again, listening and making it as sensitive as you can.

As soon as you can hear the underlying harmonies, you can make up hundreds of pieces like this. To prove it to yourself, turn the 'Trois Poules' tune into a waltz, beginning:

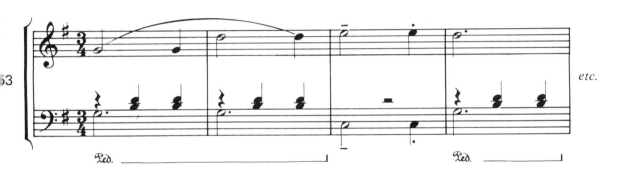

And you can imagine minor tunes in a similar way:

Hear how your pedalling follows the harmony. It will become important later.

Step 13: Chord varieties

Up till now you have used all your chords in root position (that is, growing from the root as the left hand's lowest note). Now you can change the variety of the growth by 'turning it over': musically, this is called 'inverting' chords so that they become:

INVERSIONS

A chord is in its root position when the note at the bottom carries the name of the chord. The chord of G as you have played it is:

Ex. 55

To make quite sure you can hear this, play:

1 The root position of Chord 1 in A major.
2 The root position of Chord 5 in F major.
3 The root position of Chord 4 in D major.
4 The root position of Chord 1 in G minor.
5 The root position of Chord 4 in F♯ minor.
6 The root position of Chord 5 in B minor.

Check with page 82 to make sure that your ears have given you the right answer.

Here is the chord of C again, as you have played it, but for the right hand only — without the top C:

Ex. 56

C is the root.
E is the third: an interval of a third above the root.
G is the fifth: an interval of a fifth above the root.

Remember from your work on intervals that all arithmetic in Harmony is inclusive.

How do you make the first 'inversion'?

1   Play the chord in its root position and write it down.

Ex. 57

2   Cross out the root and, instead, write it on top of the chord like this:

Ex. 58

3   Play the two chords one after the other so that you can hear the 'variety': the third of the original chord has become the lowest note of the new sound and this sound is the *first inversion* of the chord of C major.

Remember that the *chord* has not changed: you have simply inverted the notes to vary its sound.

Step 14: Labelling the varieties

Just as you practised playing all the chords in each key with the right hand alone (page 82), now practise inverting all the Chords 1, 4 and 5 in those keys, listening to the way you vary the sound. In the keys of D and its relative minor, B minor, you will start like this:

Ex. 59

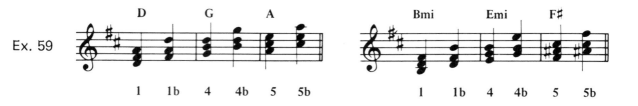

Next, again just as you did with chords originally, take the lowest note down into the left hand, so that in D major and B minor you will play:

Ex. 60

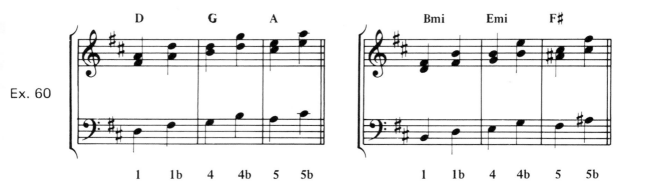

First inversions are distinguished by label 'b'.

Once you can play all the chords you know in their *first* inversions and have begun to recognise the different sound **by ear**, you can use exactly the same means to make *second* inversions. Go back to the right hand only and do as you did in Example 58:

1 Play chord C in its root position and write it down.
2 Cross out the root and write it on top of the chord.
3 Cross out the 3rd of the chord and write it on top:

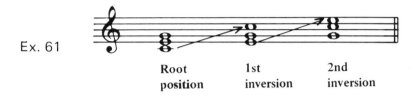

Ex. 61

Root position   1st inversion   2nd inversion

Remember that the note E is the 3rd of chord C, wherever it is; G is the 5th of chord C wherever it is. In first inversions the 3rd is the lowest note; in second inversions the 5th is the lowest note. Repeat this last sentence until you cannot ever forget it.

Now play all the chords you know with the right hand only, inverting them twice, listening to the varieties of sound. Here are two examples to start you off:

Taking the lowest note down into the left hand you will play:

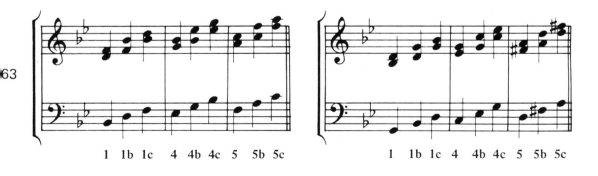

Second inversions are distinguished by the label 'c'.

There is only one other possible inversion of any chord you have learned so far and that is only possible in the chord with four different notes in it: Chord 5^7. **Chord 5^7 alone has a third inversion.** Build it as you did the others.

1 Play G^7 (Chord 5^7 in the key of C) in its root position and write it down.
2 Cross out the root and write it on top.
3 Cross out the 3rd and write *that* on top.
4 Cross out the 5th and write *that* on top:

Ex. 64

Remember that the note F is the 7th of the chord G wherever it is in the chord. In third inversions, the 7th is the lowest note. Add this last sentence to the one you memorised on page 41! Play a few chords of 5^7 with the right hand only, inverting them three times, listening to the varieties of sound. A start for you:

Ex. 65

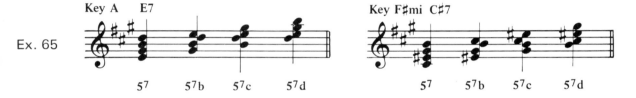

A reminder, in case you have forgotten why E is sharp (E♯) in F sharp minor in this last example: look at the harmonic minor scale of F sharp minor (page 80). You are harmonising, so you must use the harmonic minor; the melodic minor notes only apply to melodies, that is, in tune-writing.

Last, in learning *all* possible inversions, take the lowest note into the left hand again and practise a few chords like this:

Ex. 66

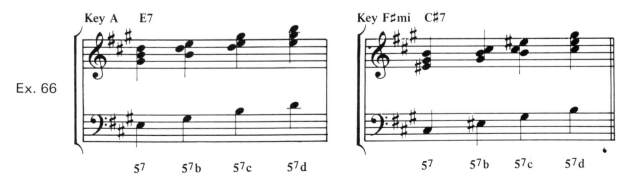

Third inversions are distinguished by the label 'd'.

The labels of all varieties of chord must be immediately understood both by your eyes and your ears. These simple rules summarise what you need to know, understand and remember:

1 The root is the note which gives its name to the chord: 1, 4, 5 or 5^7 of your present selection.
2 The 3rd is the note at an interval of a third above the root.
3 The 5th is the note at an interval of a fifth above the root.
4 Wherever they are in an inversion, the root, the 3rd note and the 5th note keep their names:

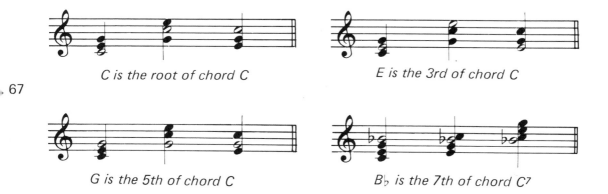

C is the root of chord C   *E is the 3rd of chord C*

67

G is the 5th of chord C   *B♭ is the 7th of chord C7*

5 To label the root, write it on every chord: 1, 4 or 5.
6 To label a first inversion, use 'b' = 1b or 4b or 5b.
7 To label a second inversion, use 'c' = 1c or 4c or 5c.
8 To label a third inversion (only obtainable from 5^7 chords as yet), use 'd' = 5^7d.

Never confuse keys and chords.

To test your understanding of this:

In the *key* of G, Chord 4 is C–E–G–C = chord C is 4 in G
In the *key* of C, Chord 1 is C–E–G–C = chord C is 1 in C
In the *key* of F, Chord 5 is C–E–G–C = chord C is 5 in F

Look back at the labels on Examples 46 to 66 and the method should be clear. As another game, play a mixture of chords into your cassette recorder. Keep a note of their labels. Play back and ask your ear to recognise them. If you have anyone else learning with you, simply try this out on one another.

Interlude III

You have learned how to hear major and minor scales; how to distinguish keys from one another; how to build Chords 1, 4 and 5 in any key; how to begin to give these chords a 'pianistic' sound; and in the last step, how to give yourself a wider variety of sounds within these three chords, by inversion.

From the equipment of 'playing by ear' you can recognise and use:

KEYS
INTERVALS
COMMON CHORDS

You should by now be able to recognise inversions: so you can learn how to use them and how to begin introducing less common chords.

Before you go on to apply the knowledge you have acquired since the last 'Interlude', check that your ear understands what your brain has told it from Steps 6–14.

Step 15: Using inversions

To vary a harmonisation with inversions, look again at an 'all-root' harmonisation such as you can now do:

Ex. 68

Play these eight bars and decide with your ear where an inversion might sound better than a root position, still using the basic chords (1, 4, 5, 5^7). This may sound hard to do but, as in previous steps, a lot can be done by deduction and by a keen ear.

Do you notice that in the first two bars Chord 1 is repeated in root position? Here may be a chance to give the harmony some variety by inverting the chord in one of these bars. Ask yourself:

1 Which of these chords might have the 'inversion'?
2 Which inversion might you use? First or second inversion?

Bar 1: The key of G is clear to the ear from using Chord 1. So why not leave it there?
Bar 2: The same chord is repeated. What about a first inversion of Chord 1: Chord 1b?

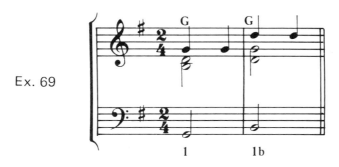

Ex. 69

If you play the chords in this example *without* the tune, you have the progression you have practised in Example 58. Putting the tune on top gives you four-note chords

45

again. But notice how wide the stretch of your right hand is, in Chord 1b. If the tune had a G at the top, the stretch for a good sound would still be the same:

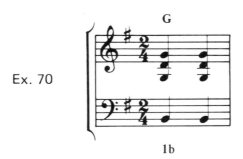

Ex. 70

Remember that in first inversions, your right hand should be stretched to eight notes (an octave) with one note in between completing the chord. Try this with as many first inversions as you can, like this, moving about the piano in Chords 1b after root positions.

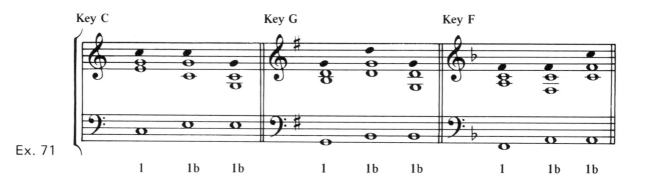

Ex. 71

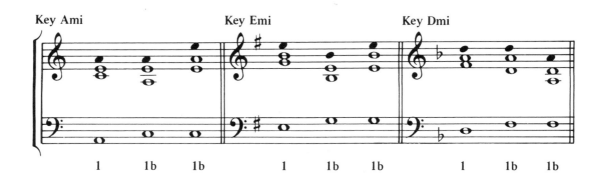

Think of the black noteheads as the tune in each case so that you begin to hear *downwards*: you are adding one left hand note (the 'bass' as you will know it from now on) and two other right-hand notes to complete the labelled chords.

Bar 3: The chord is Chord 4 in root position. There is little to be gained from changing it.

Never invert a chord for the sake of being clever or 'original'. Music is most effective when it is direct and economic in harmony.

Bar 4: This uses Chord 1, root position, a very final sound. As this is only the middle of an eight-bar phrase, an inversion might be better.

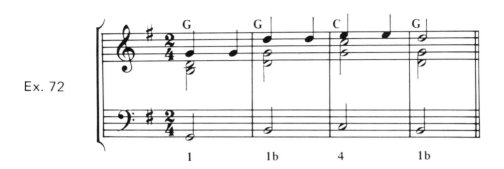

Ex. 72

As always, only hear your harmonies **related to each other** and not in isolation. You can't really decide whether you like Chord 1b here until you complete the rest. Often in playing by ear you have to put the cart before the horse, thinking ahead. With this in mind, sing the last four bars to yourself and work backwards.

Bar 8: To end a phrase it is usually more pleasing to the ear to use a root position unless you want to 'leave the sound in the air'. So aim at the root in bar 8.

Bar 7: This is a nice, rich 5^7, so why change it? Try 5^7b for fun and see if you like it; if not, stick to the roots.

Bar 6: 1b won't work for most ears. But *try*; and hear what the sound lacks. You may even like it and only *your* ear can judge.

Bar 5: Here, with Chord 4, you can add variety by using 4b:

Ex. 73

Now try all the chords in bars 5 to 8 in their context:

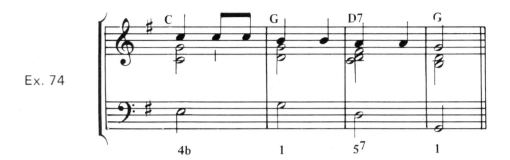

Ex. 74

Although you know how to make second inversions you have not used them so far. In fact, they are rare, but most valued — like so many things — *because* they are rare. The main thing to know is that a second inversion usually likes to be on the first beat of a bar; and that it is best to plant it firmly with bass notes on the same note, on either side (or only one step away). Looking at the bass of the last example, the only places where a bass note *could* have a note either side on the same note or one step away are in bars 3, 4 and 6.

A second inversion on C in bar 3 would not include the tune note: in bar 4, a second inversion on D would be possible; but a second inversion on D in bar 6 would settle most happily.

Ex. 75

Try substituting these second inversions in bars 3, 4 and 6 by ear, one by one, and hear the effect for yourself.

As for a third inversion — only possible at present on 5^7 — try it in bar 7 and see if you like it in its context of bars 5 to 8.

It's really an exotic variety but you will find a use for it some time later!

Going back to the minor tune, what different varieties of inversion can you mix in? Simply try inverting every chord in turn and hear what effect it has. To save time — though by now you will know that patience is vital — here are the first inversions of your three chords in another 'swinging' rhythm exercise:

Ex. 76

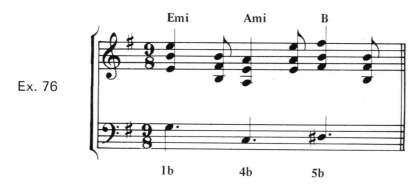

and here are the second inversion possibilities:

Ex. 77

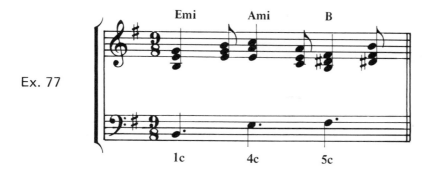

If you want a clue, try looking at the last two bars where you can mix first and second inversions:

Ex. 78

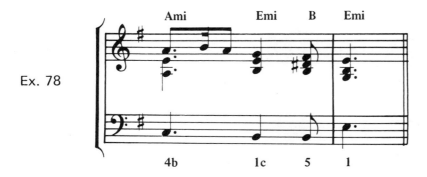

Step 16: Complete harmonisations

By the time you can play Chords 1, 4, 5 and 5^7 with their inversions by ear, in major and minor keys with up to three flats and three sharps in the key-signature, you will know how to use all the basic tools in the equipment. All other harmony only extends this knowledge and it is vital that you can use these basic chords to harmonise *any* tune that stays in one key before you take the next steps.

Here are basic harmonisations of the two example tunes. Read them and play them silently (on a table top if you like) whilst you try to hear them. Make sure that you know what the figures underneath mean and that the guitar chord names match your knowledge. You will notice that the chords of 'We Three Kings' are broken up in a more pianistic way.

'Quand Trois Poules'

Ex. 79

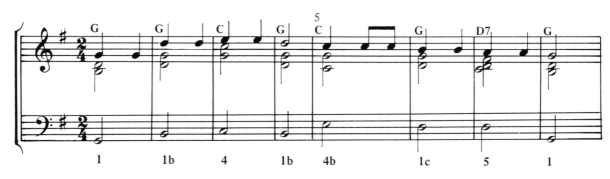

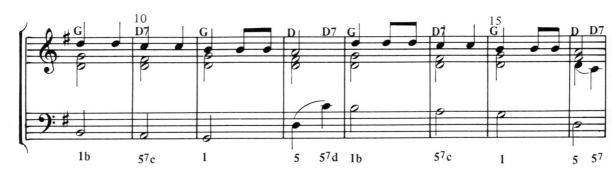

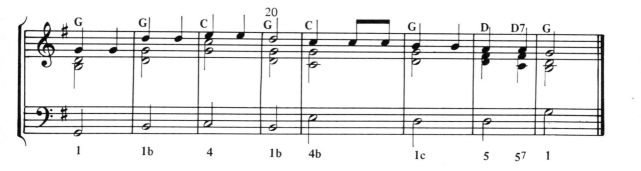

'We Three Kings'

Learn the two pieces by understanding and through your ears. It doesn't matter if you don't manage all the notes exactly as they are written but you *must* keep within the harmony. As long as you have the basic chords firmly in your ears you can't go wrong.

When you can play them easily, start asking questions about the harmony. In 'Quand Trois Poules': compare the *right* hand of bars 5 to 8 with bars 21 to 24. The chords are the same as the guitar symbols easily show and the positions are the same as the figures underneath show BUT at the end the right hand holds back the seventh (D7). What effect does this have? It heralds the ending by 'thickening' the sound.

Now look at the left hand of bar 12. Here the left hand holds back the seventh (D^7). What effect does this have? Because the right hand chord is a long one, the left hand keeps the music going. Lastly, look at the *right* hand again in bar 16. Here again, playing the seventh note (C) on the second beat keeps things moving. Practise doing this with ends of phrases in several keys, like this:

Ex. 81

Begin to take a broad view of a whole tune before you start harmonising, work at least in whole phrases and no longer from bar to bar. This was essential to begin with, but now your ears need stretching just as your fingers did when you practised inversions.

The purpose of making things more pianistic is to **keep things moving**. Notice again how the harmony is filled out at the end in the right hand of Example 79 and how the left hand provides the finishing touches with a 'broken' chord figure in Example 80. The rest of the harmonies in Example 80 — because this is piano music — are also broken up as you have the pedal to help you. Change the pedal carefully exactly where it is shown.

Always change the pedal when the harmony changes.

Your new understanding and your ear will tell you *when* the harmony changes; clear pedalling is essential.

Four more suggestions for you to harmonise. Modelled on 'Quand Trois Poules': 'Good King Wenceslas' in G and 'Frère Jacques' in F. Modelled on 'We Three Kings': 'Greensleeves' in E minor and 'Charlie is my darling' in D minor (first half). *After* you have made yours up, compare with the versions on pages 85 to 87.

Step 17: Growing chords 3

You understand the relationship between major and minor keys. The same relationship applies to Chords 1, 4 and 5. When you first thought of these three chords as a family (mother, son or daughter, and father, in Step 6) they formed the inner family circle. Each, however, has a 'cousin' able to take his or her place on many occasions. To refresh your memory, write out the scales and chords of C major and G major, labelling Chords 2, 3 and 6:

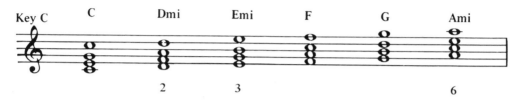

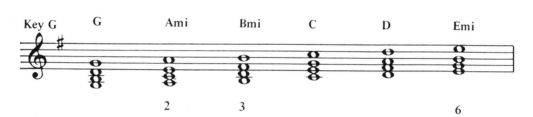

Have a good look at them. Can you see who is related to whom? Not immediately, perhaps. Look at Chord 2 in C: using guitar symbols, the chord of D minor. What is the relative major of D minor? F major. Which chord in the key of C is F major? Chord 4. Therefore, Chord 2 is the 'cousin' of Chord 4.

Read the last paragraph again, looking at the example. When you are sure you understand, ask yourself — first in the key of C:

1   What is Chord 3 in guitar terms? E minor.
2   What is the relative major of E minor? G major.
3   Which chord in this key is G? Chord 5.

So Chord 3 is the 'cousin' of Chord 5. Test this in the key of G by asking the same questions again, looking at the second part of the example. Now apply the same deductions to Chord 6. Chord 6 is related to . . .? Chord 1.

Check that you understand the nature of this relationship, which is vital to extending your range of harmony.

Step 18: Using the cousins

Here is 'Polly Put the Kettle on' harmonised with Chords 1, 4, 5 and 5^7.

Try playing Chord 2 whenever there is Chord 4 (bars 7, 11 and 15). This will give you:

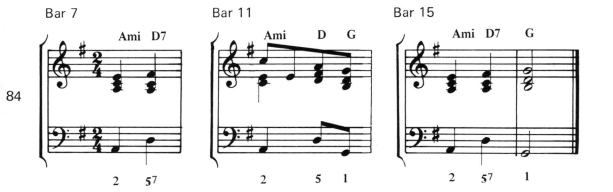

Your ear will tell you that this sound is more satisfactory.

In the same way, try to introduce Chord 6 into the harmonisation.

The 'cousins' are taking the place of the 'inner family' to form a more colourful sound. Sometimes the Chords 2, 3 and 6 fit in well; sometimes they don't.

If you listen carefully, your ear will tell you where the cousins can be used.

This comes with practice.

What deductions can you make about Chords 2, 3 and 6?

1   They are all minor chords and can often replace Chords 1, 4 and 5. You can think of them as coming in to help out.
2   A tune in a major key needs to be 'at home' as soon as possible and none of the Chords 2, 3 or 6 is a 'home' chord.
3   A tune needs to come home at the end and no full ending can be trusted to Chords 2, 3 or 6.
4   If you use them too often, the music will go 'minor'; though you may enjoy this as a change, it can also sound weak and sad.

Apply these deductions to your harmony and see if you can come up with something like the one on page 88.

You have used the 'cousins' as substitutes. But they can sometimes sound well entirely in themselves. Bar 3 in Example 83 still sounded dull.

What cousin uses A? Play from the beginning and try Chord 2; it fits, but the move from Chord 1 to Chord 2 is jerky. Play from the beginning and try Chord 2b; Better?

5   Beware of Chords 1 and 2 next to each other in root position: always try inverting one of them for a smoother sound (1 − 2b or 1b − 2).

Remember that cousins are inverted in the same way as the inner family. In the key of C:

Ex. 85

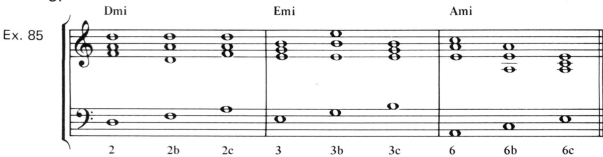

In the key of D:

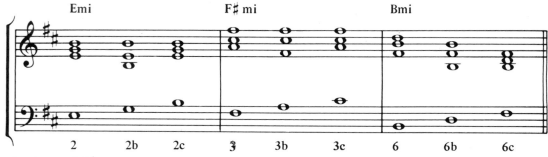

In the key of B♭:

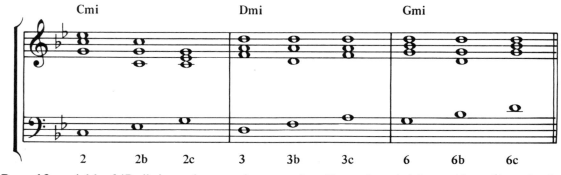

Bars 10 and 11 of 'Polly' can be much smoother if you heed this caution. Now look at the **final** harmonisation on page 88 and play it many times to appreciate *how* it was built up, referring back to the whole of this step.

Interlude IV

Chords have now grown from every root but one in the scales you began with in the first Step. The variety may well bewilder you, particularly as you use Chords 2, 3 and 6 in inversions. You have already come across a 'formula' for a particular piano sound (page 52). For fun, practise the harmonic 'formula' which makes the last three bars of 'Polly' as you have just played it:

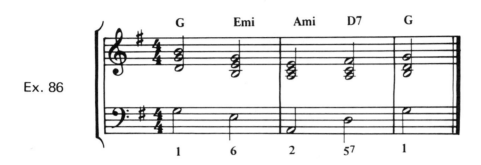

Ex. 86

Then split the beats and you will have the most popular formula of all time in 'light' music.

Ex. 87

Or, in waltz time:

88

Try singing some tunes on top of the accompaniment, then try to play the harmonies all with your left hand and pick out the tune on top. Here are a few tunes to go on with: (Ends of phrases may need the formula you have already used in 'Quand Trois Poules'.)

These Foolish Things
Amazing Grace
Auld Lang Syne
Loch Lomond
Downtown
Blue Moon
All through the night
Cockles and Mussels
Singing in the Rain
Will ye no come back again?

Perhaps all the work on chords isn't so dull, after all?

Step 19: Changing keys 1

Formulas may be fun but they can be very frustrating, as many a beginner learning to play by ear *only* from formulas finds to his cost. Even good jazz musicians who seem to play marvellously by ear from well-used formulas grow exasperated as they search for some new sound because they do not know **how** the chords they use are made up.

To remind yourself of the variety available beyond the formula you have just tried, try 'Loch Lomond' in G and 'Auld Lang Syne' in F. Experiment until you find a way to use *at least one* of each chord (1 to 6) in each harmonisation. It may help to write down at least the tune and the bass of your harmonisation as it begins to make musical sense to you, so that you don't forget what you did as you get nearer the end.

But

Do not cheat by copying tunes from books; even if you only know part of a tune it will be enough to practise harmonising. The harmonisations at the back of the book are there so that you will only look at them *after* you have made up your own, for comparison. The order of all your experiments should be: ears, fingers, ears, eyes. And the eyes are only to see what you have played by ear as you write it down. Now you can look at page 89 to see and hear possible harmonisations of 'Loch Lomond' and 'Auld Lang Syne' using all the available chords.

The worst frustration about a formula is that tunes seldom stay in the same key all the time and the formula won't survive the change. How many times do you forget the middle of a popular tune?

Staying in one key, you use only the chords of that 'family'. In music, as in life, a family will usually visit relations, and in music, as you have heard, the nearest relations to major keys are their minors. So major keys sometimes 'visit' their minor relatives and minor relatives visit their majors.

Can you remember the chorus of 'We Three Kings'? Sing it, and write the tune only on the end of your harmonisation in Step 10. Here are bars 5 to 10:

Ex. 89

If you play the rest of the chorus your ear will tell you that it is undoubtedly in G major. You started in E minor so there is a change of key: the minor is visiting the major relative . . . and in this case, stays there! Your only concern is to find the way it goes. The beginning of bar 8 is in E minor but by bar 9 you are in G. The route is very short . . . in fact, the one note marked *. The chord you use for this note is the link between the two keys. The note may suggest Chord 1, 3 or 5 in G major. Try each chord in turn.

Which makes the best link? D.

Ex. 90

Again, the change of chords in bar 8 sounds jerky. Like changing gear in a car, changing keys in music should be smooth.

60

Chord 7

You will have noticed by now that no mention has been made of the chord on the seventh of any scale. Your chords have been restricted to 1, 2, 3, 4, 5, 5^7 and 6 with their inversions. This is because Chord 7 is 'irregular' and does not fit in well with the family. In G major it *looks* like this:

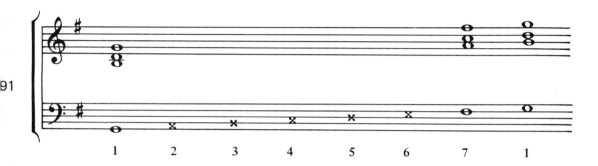

Play it and ask yourself: is it a major or a minor chord? All the rest are one or the other; Chord 7 is neither. In fact you can regard it as the 'uncle' you rarely see! But if you use the Chord 5^7b on the seventh note, you have the most useful chord of all in changing keys. Try it on 'We Three Kings'.

and hear the smooth gear-change!

Build chords on the seventh note of the major scales with up to three sharps or flats in them but make them 5^7b. Check what they look like after you have found them by ear (page 90).

Build chords on the seventh note of harmonic minor scales with up to three sharps or flats in their key-signatures, again making them 5^7b. Check them with page 90.

In this first key-change, E minor 'visited' G major and stayed. Look back at bars 5 to 6 in the tune. It is quite possible for E minor to pay a quick visit **and return** in these two bars. Experiment by ear and harmonise both these bars in G. Write your harmonisation of the whole tune down and compare it with page 91.

Step 20: Changing keys 2

Most families have friends living nearby whom they visit frequently; those living a long distance away do not receive as many visits. With musical families of keys, the nearby friends are those with one sharp or one flat more *or* less in their key signatures.

Look at the Family Circle you met, on page 8. In *sharp* keys, C is nearby G (which has one sharp more). In *flat* keys, C is nearby F (which has one flat more). In sharp keys, D is near G (which has one sharp less) *and* A (which has one sharp more). In flat keys B♭ is near F (which has one flat less) *and* E♭ (which has one flat more).

Work out the remaining nearby keys for yourself. The same goes for minor keys: one flat or sharp more *or* less in the key-signatures tells you how nearby the keys are.

Test what your eyes and brain have worked out, with your ears. Play the tune of 'Billy Boy' in F, write it down, and compare it with page 92 to check that you have it right. Which nearby key does it visit in bars 6 and 7? C major (one flat less). The 'foreign' note B♮ gave the game away. But now play 'Barbara Allen' in D, write it down and compare it with page 92.

Play it several times. Listen carefully, particularly to bars 3 and 4. Do you hear a change? The melody sounds as if it is pulling away from the key and being drawn towards another. It could settle in A (one sharp more than D). Here you can test yourself by using the Chord 5⁷b in A somewhere in those two bars. Play the notes of this 'link' chord; if you're stuck, refer to the example on page 90. Harmonise the tune from the beginning and use the link chord in bar 3. The key is changed and the visit made . . . briefly, though, as bar 5 hears you back in D (no note of G♯).

You could not have *seen* this change from looking at the tune (which has no notes 'foreign' to D major); you can only *hear* it.

The Chord 5⁷b is not, of course, the only link chord. In many cases, a chord is common to two keys and will form a link quite naturally. Probably the most useful of these common links are chords 6 and 2. This shows how one chord becomes another as you change key:

Key C

Ex. 93

6

Key G

So the chord of A minor becomes a link between the keys of C and G:

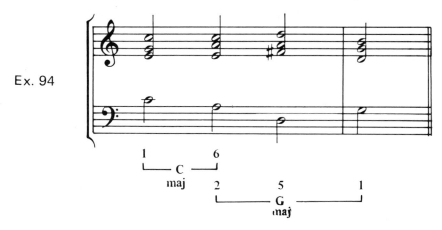

Ex. 94

As soon as you have used the link chord, bring in the note which separates the keys (in this case a sharp, F♯). A useful hint is:

1   When you want to change to a *sharper* key, Chord 6 in your home key is a good link.

Applying the same deduction, you will find

2   When you want to change to a *flatter* key, Chord 2 in your home key is a good link.

So the chord of D minor becomes a link between the keys of C and F:

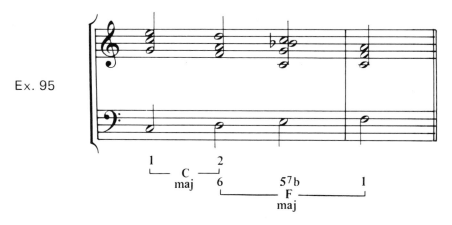

Ex. 95

Do you remember that when the 'cousin' chords were mentioned, they were described as being helpful. They certainly are when visiting neighbouring keys. You could regard these members of the family as links with the outside world.

63

Step 21: Using the links

Pick out the tune of 'The Ash Grove' in G. Write it down until it returns home (that is, when the first bars start again). Check your version with page 92. Play bars 13 to 16 and ask:

1   What is the change of key? G to D, a sharper key.
2   What is the link chord for sharper keys? Chord 6 in the home key.
3   What is Chord 6 in the home key (answer in guitar terms)? E minor.

Put question and answer into practice and you will play something like:

Ex 96

The link chord has done its job in belonging to both keys and the new key has really 'moved in' with its three basic chords (4, 5^7, 1 in D). Try harmonising the whole tune and then compare yours with page 93.

Now try the whole of 'Barbara Allen' in D. If you can't remember the tune, you will find it on page 92. Play bars 3 and 4, asking yourself the same questions as you did above for 'The Ash Grove'. The link chord will be chord 6 in D, B minor, like this:

Ex. 97

Try harmonising the whole tune and then compare yours with page 94.

64

Make up a tune, starting with four bars in F major and going in the next four bars to B flat major, in ¾ time. Do *not* use this but write down something like it:

1 What is the link chord for flatter keys? Chord **2** in the home key.
2 What is Chord 2 in the home key? G minor.

Now harmonise your tune with a chord of G minor as a link.

You will not find many short tunes changing to flatter keys. The usual place to find 'flatter' changes is just before the end: the move to the flat side then makes the ending seem brighter.

Remember:

1 That you need Chords 4, 5 and 1 in the new key before you have fully changed keys. Chords 5 and 1 are not enough to convince the ear that you have moved altogether . . . but they are good enough for a fleeting visit.

2 That there may *or may not* be a common linking chord such as Chord 6 or 2 in the home key.

and, from Step 19 on page 61:

3 That 5⁷b into the new key is easy to use.

Interlude V

With all the knowledge of scales, chords and keys up to now firmly in your head and in your ears, backed up with the look of them on paper, you should be able to play almost anything by ear. The remaining pages are ways of embellishing the basic harmony — called in music 'decoration' — and of branching out into 'free' improvisation by decorating a tune framework. The better your technique the more adventurous you can become in all styles.

Step 22: Decoration 1

You have already come across a chord with an added note – Chord 5^7 – in which the added seventh 'decorates' the original harmony. A decorated chord sounds richer than its straightforward root but, as in any concoction, it is possible to make the whole thing *too* rich.

Be economic in using added notes so that you do not overload the music with decoration. As you have already met 5^7, experiment by 'adding' sevenths on the basic Chords 1 and 4. In the key of C, this will give you (straightforward chord first):

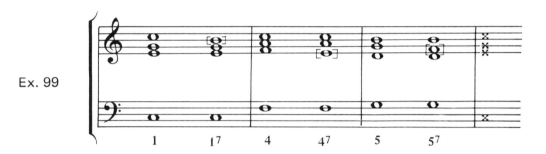

Ex. 99

The added seventh is marked [   ] in each case. Do the chords of 1^7 and 4^7 sound 'spicy' rather than richer?

There *is* a difference in sound. Now add sevenths on the remaining 'useful' chords of C major: 2^7, 3^7 and 6^7.

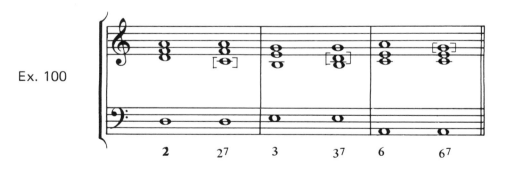

Ex. 100

They are nearer the sound of 5^7 but, of course, the basic chords of 2, 3 and 6 are minor chords to begin with, so the sound is still not exactly the same. All your ear will tell you is that 1^7 and 4^7 are very different because the 'added seventh' is a major seventh; the others are minor sevenths.

Guitarists recognise the difference by using exact terminology, and keyboard numbers using + signs can have the same meaning.

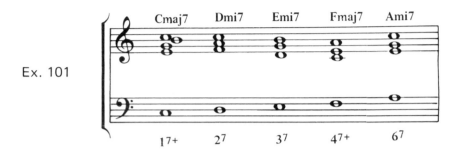

Ex. 101

Choose either way but remember: minor sevenths on Chords 2, 3, and 6 have a sound different from the major sevenths on Chords 1 and 4.

Experiment with added sevenths to any of your harmonisations until you can choose *by ear* when they sound good and when they are 'overloading' the harmony. Very often they have a 'softening' effect.

A favourite chord in the 1920s and 1930s was one with an 'added sixth', particularly on the major Chords 1 and 4. In E♭ major:

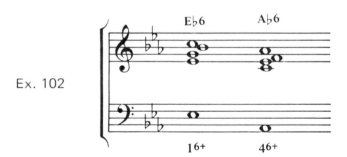

Ex. 102

Play several 'added sixths' on Chords 1 and 4 in keys up to three flats or three sharps. After a while, your ears will remember:

1. Chords 1 and 4 can quite often be decorated with an added *sixth*.
2. Chords 2, 3 and 7 can quite often be decorated with an added *seventh*.
3. Chord 5^7 is so usual that it can *very* often be used.

Try decorating the formula from Example 86, remembering these three points:

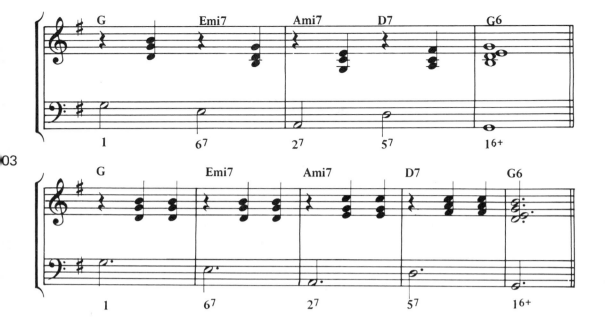

03

Notice how the right hand can re-arrange the notes of the chords as you want to hear them. Listen carefully to the added notes as you play so that you will always know the effect *with* or *without* them. *Never over-do decoration.* It is a matter of taste. Sometimes you want rich decoration, sometimes 'spice' and sometimes – most times – just simplicity.

There is one more exotic decoration to your basic chords: the added ninth. This can be added to any chord (1 to 6) as your ear wishes. Here are a few at random to set your fingers and ears working:

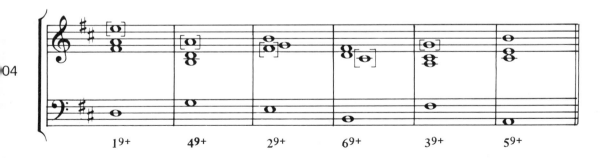

04

Again, some are 'spicy', some are richer. The most often added *ninths* are those on the chords usually happy with added *sevenths*. You have learnt that 5^7 is in fact a commonly-used chord. Now play 5^7 with an added ninth in keys up to three sharps or three flats, starting in A major:

Ex. 105

The pianist has to spend time finding out and getting used to these chords. The guitarist is so used to it that he simply calls it 'E^9', knowing that he will *also* play the added seventh.

Now decorate the other 'rich' chords with added sevenths (2 and 6) *also* with added ninths. Here they are in B flat:

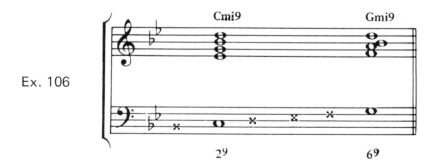

Ex. 106

A last pointer:

1   Chords 2^7 and 6^7 can often be decorated further with added ninths.
2   Chord 5^7 can have an added ninth as well, except at the end of a phrase.
3   Chords 1, 3 and 5 can be 'spiced' with added ninths.

So that you can hear how even a simple tune like 'Quand Trois Poules' can be decorated to appear in disguise with added-note chords, try as many as you can in the harmonisation you already have. Page 95 gives you a most exotic result.

Step 23: Decoration 2

You began by picking out tunes. Once you are also able to play all the harmonies at your disposal by ear and understanding, it is time to return to tunes and hear how to decorate them, too.

From the beginning you have been urged not to harmonise every note of a tune. With a richly decorated tune, it is simply impossible to harmonise every note.

Here is the same tune *without* these 'decorating' notes; and you will see how the bones of the tune are the essential part of it. These essential notes are the ones that need to be harmonised.

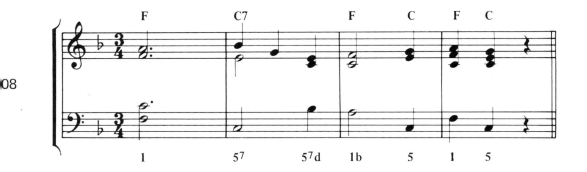

The 'decorating' notes pass the ears so quickly that their clash with the harmony is unnoticed: so they are called 'passing notes'.

Although this may seem far removed from the adventure of playing by ear, it is very much, in fact, a part of it. When you are harmonising a tune at the keyboard it is important to recognise which notes of the melody are the ones to harmonise and which are the ones best left without chords.

Some passing notes have a special stress (*accented* passing notes) often because they occur on a strong beat, and they steal the chord really belonging to an essential melody note.

Here are the last four bars of the tune 'Early One Morning', in D major:

Ex. 109

If you play this over, paying attention to bar 2 of the phrase, you will hear that in this bar the C♯ and the A want to resolve on to the respective notes that follow them. This should give you a clue to the fact that there are stressed notes lurking in this bar. In other words, the C♯ sounds as if it wants to *resolve* on to the next note, B, instead of merely being followed by it. Therefore, the C♯ is a stressed passing note, and it occurs on the strong beat of the bar.

To harmonise effectively we have to determine the difference between passing notes and *accented* passing notes.

Here is the four-bar phrase harmonised, and you will see how the two stressed passing notes – the C♯ and the A – steal the chords from the 'essential' melody notes, B and G:

Ex. 110

A stressed passing note is a 'foreigner' to the chord and the harmony. It gives the effect of holding the music up until the accented passing note resolves on to the note that 'fits' the actual harmony. It gives a suspended feeling **to the** music.

In this Step you have alerted your ears to the difference between *inessential* passing notes and *accented* passing notes. Try harmonising **some** of the tunes you know already, using fewer harmonies and hearing how **many** notes you can make into passing notes. Working the other way round, which **of the** passing notes in Example 107 are unaccented and which accented?

Once your ear has registered these distinctions you will understand a lot more about what seems to be strange harmony in pieces you are learning to play from published music. (Example 107 was from Mozart's *Cosi fan Tutte*.)

Step 24: Going pianistic 2

Look back at Step 12, the halfway stage in the book. There you learnt the simplest way of keeping piano music going by broken chords and using the left hand to keep rhythmic interest. You should apply the extra knowledge of harmony and decoration you now have, to every piece of music you play from the copy.

Take note by ear of every harmony you come across in Haydn, Mozart, Beethoven, Schubert, Chopin, and Debussy; analyse it and add it to your repertoire of chords and finger-patterns.

Here are some examples to show you the way:

Ex. 111

Ex 112

Sonata in B♭, K.333

Mozart

Ex. 113

Sonata in G, Op. 14 No. 2

Beethoven

Sonata in A, D.664

Schubert

Prelude No. 7, Op. 28

Chopin

Ex 115

Ex. 116

Arabesque No. 1   Debussy

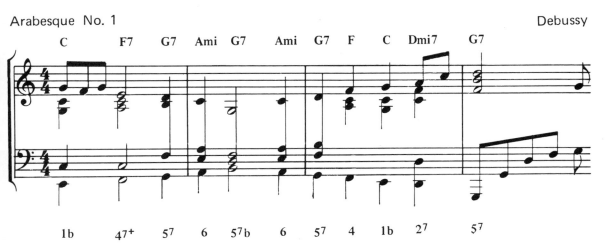

You should be able to hear these extracts with a new awareness that will make playing any written piece as much pleasure as 'playing by ear'.

Answers and Exercises

STEP 1

Scale of C

C major

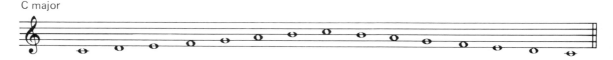

Major Scales up to Three Sharps

G major

D major

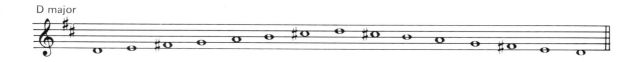

A major

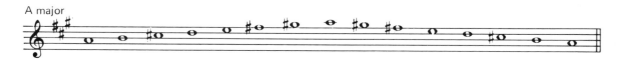

Major Scales up to Three Flats

F major

B♭ major

E♭ major

STEP 2

Scale of A minor

A harmonic minor

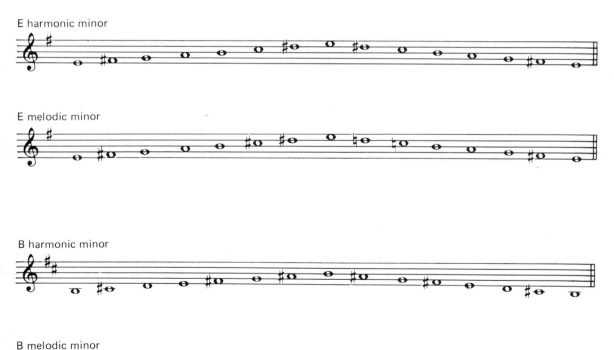

A melodic minor

Minor Scales: Key Signatures up to Three Sharps

E harmonic minor

E melodic minor

B harmonic minor

B melodic minor

F♯ harmonic minor

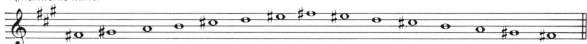

F♯ melodic minor

Minor Scales: Key Signatures up to Three Flats

D harmonic minor

D melodic minor

G harmonic minor

G melodic minor

C harmonic minor

C melodic minor

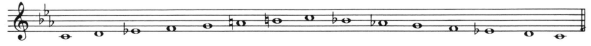

STEP 3

Answer: The intervals are a 3rd, 5th and 4th respectively.

STEP 4

Answer (a): The key would have been B minor.

Answer (b): The key is F major.

STEP 6

G major

D major

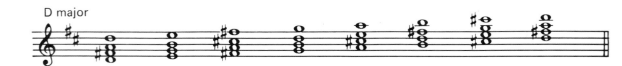

A major

F major

B♭ major

E♭ major

STEP 6: Bass Chords

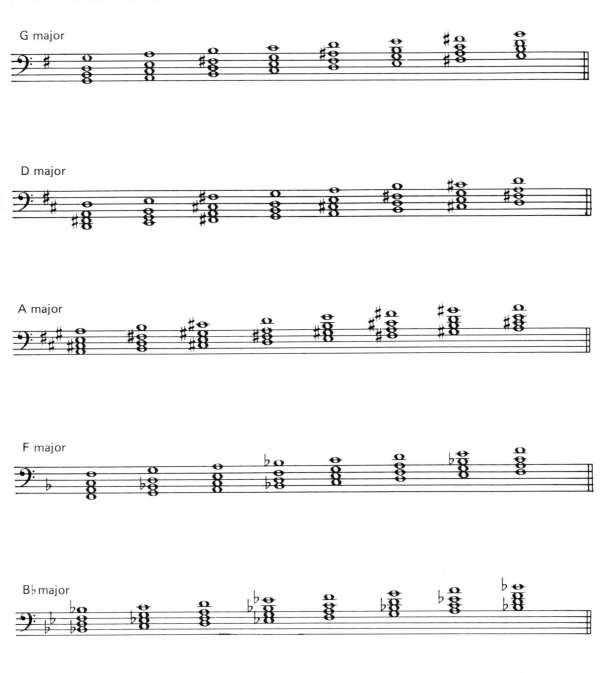

STEP 8

'Quand Trois Poules'

Bars 1 to 8, using chords 1, 4 and 5 only

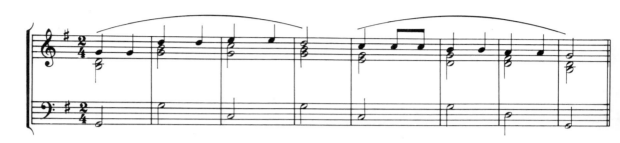

STEP 13

Answers:

1   The root position of Chord 1 in A major

2   The root position of Chord 5 in F major

3   The root position of Chord 4 in D major

4   The root position of Chord 1 in G minor

5   The root position of Chord 4 in F♯ minor

6   The root position of Chord 5 in B minor

'Good King Wenceslas'

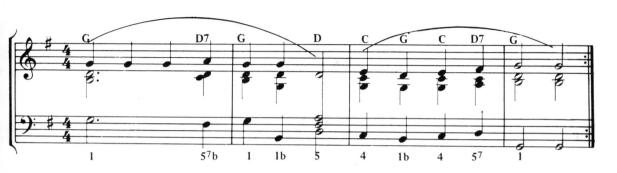

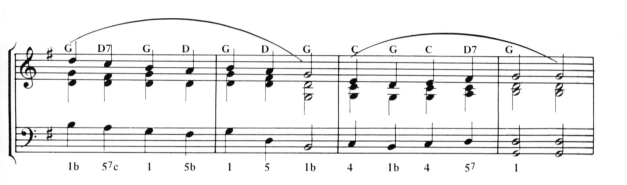

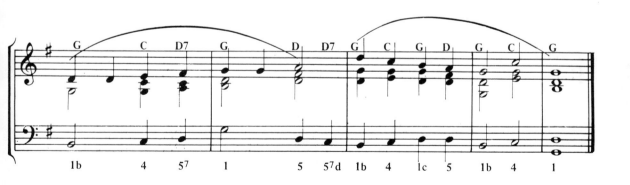

'Frère Jacques'

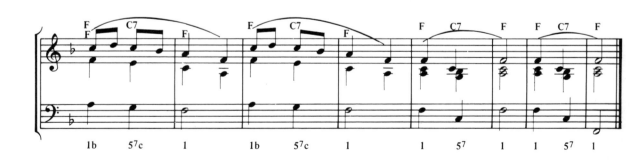

'Greensleeves'

'Charlie is my darling'

STEP 18

'Polly Put the Kettle on'

STEP 19

'Loch Lomond'

'Auld Lang Syne'

STEP 19 (CONTINUED)

Chords of 5⁷b: Major Keys

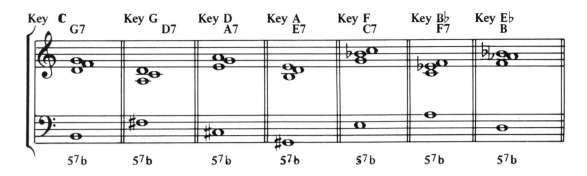

Chords of 5⁷b: Minor Keys

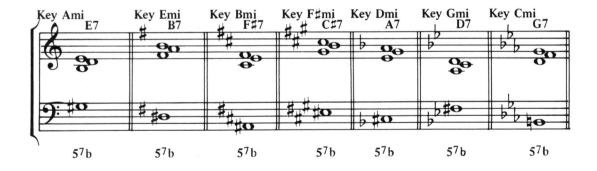

'We Three Kings'

STEP 20

'Billy Boy'

'Barbara Allen'

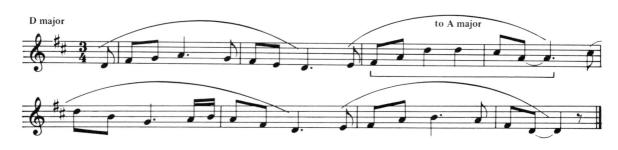

STEP 21

'The Ash Grove'

'The Ash Grove' Harmonised

'Barbara Allen' Harmonised

D ← 6 = 2 → A

STEP 22

'Quand Trois Poules' with added-note harmonies

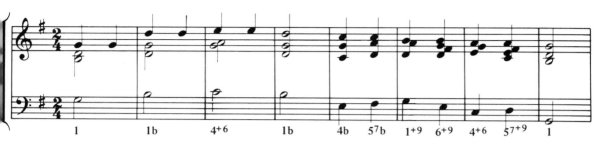

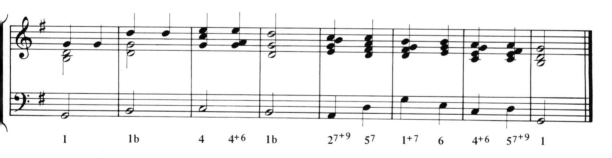